What feels hot?

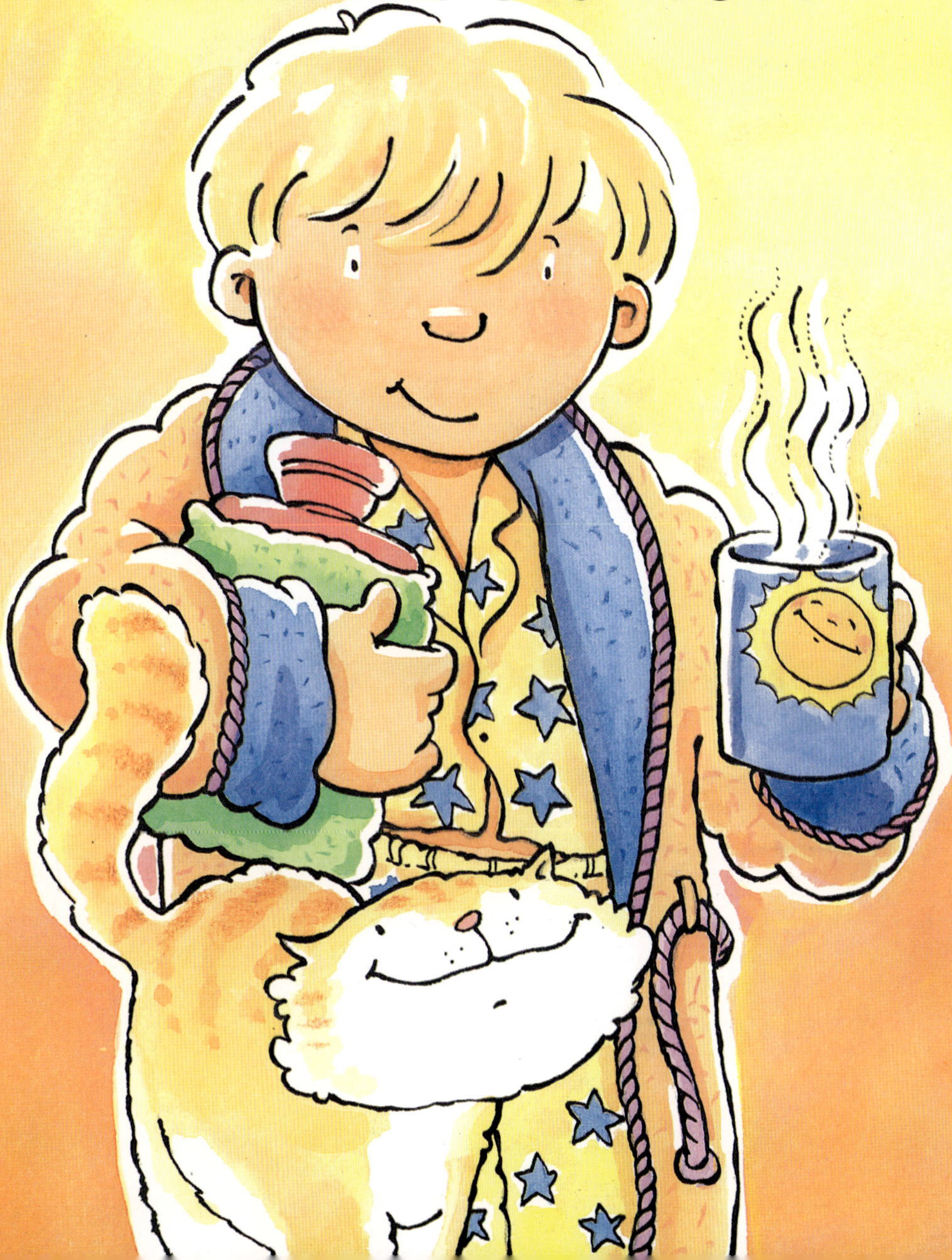

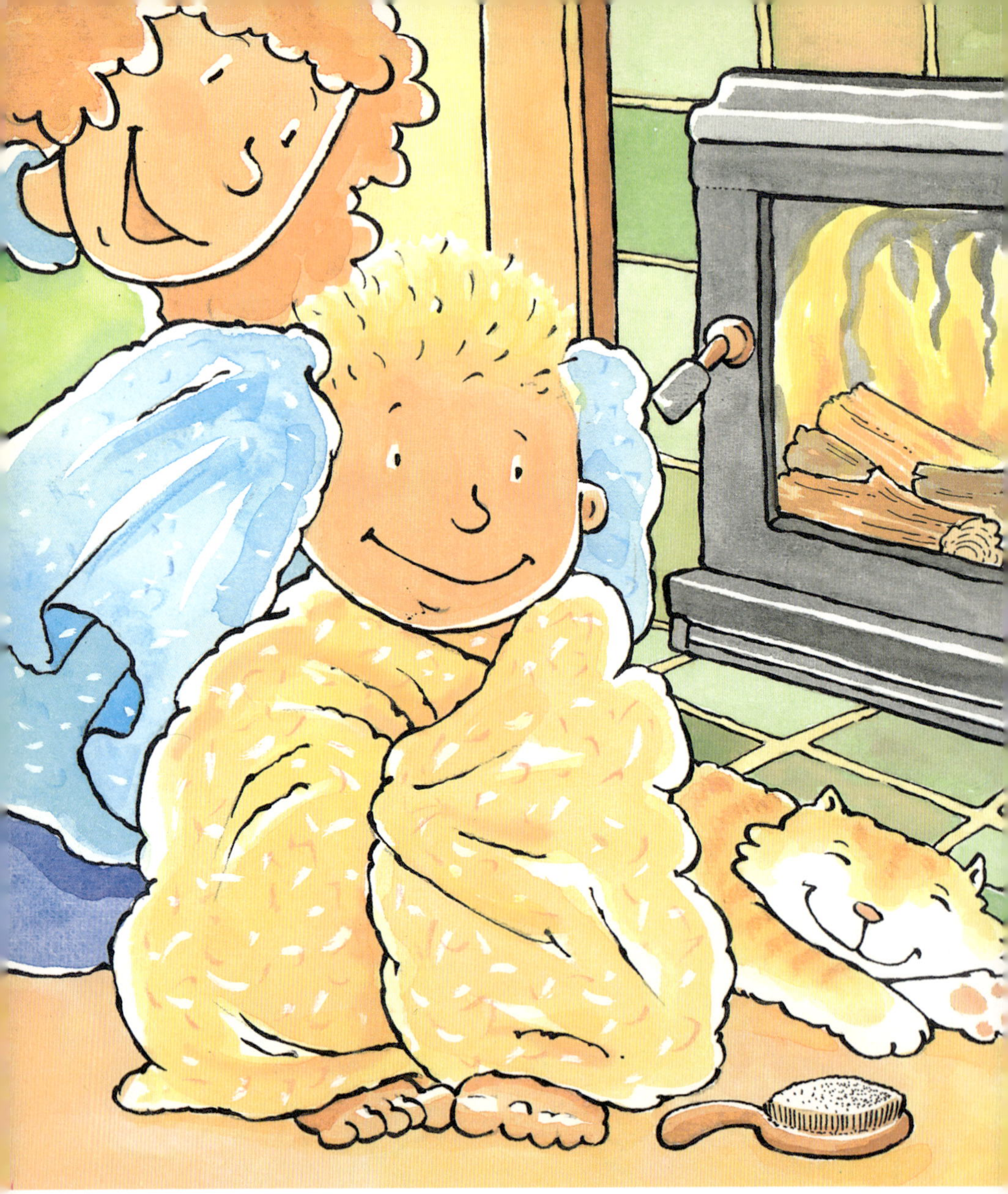

A fire is hot.

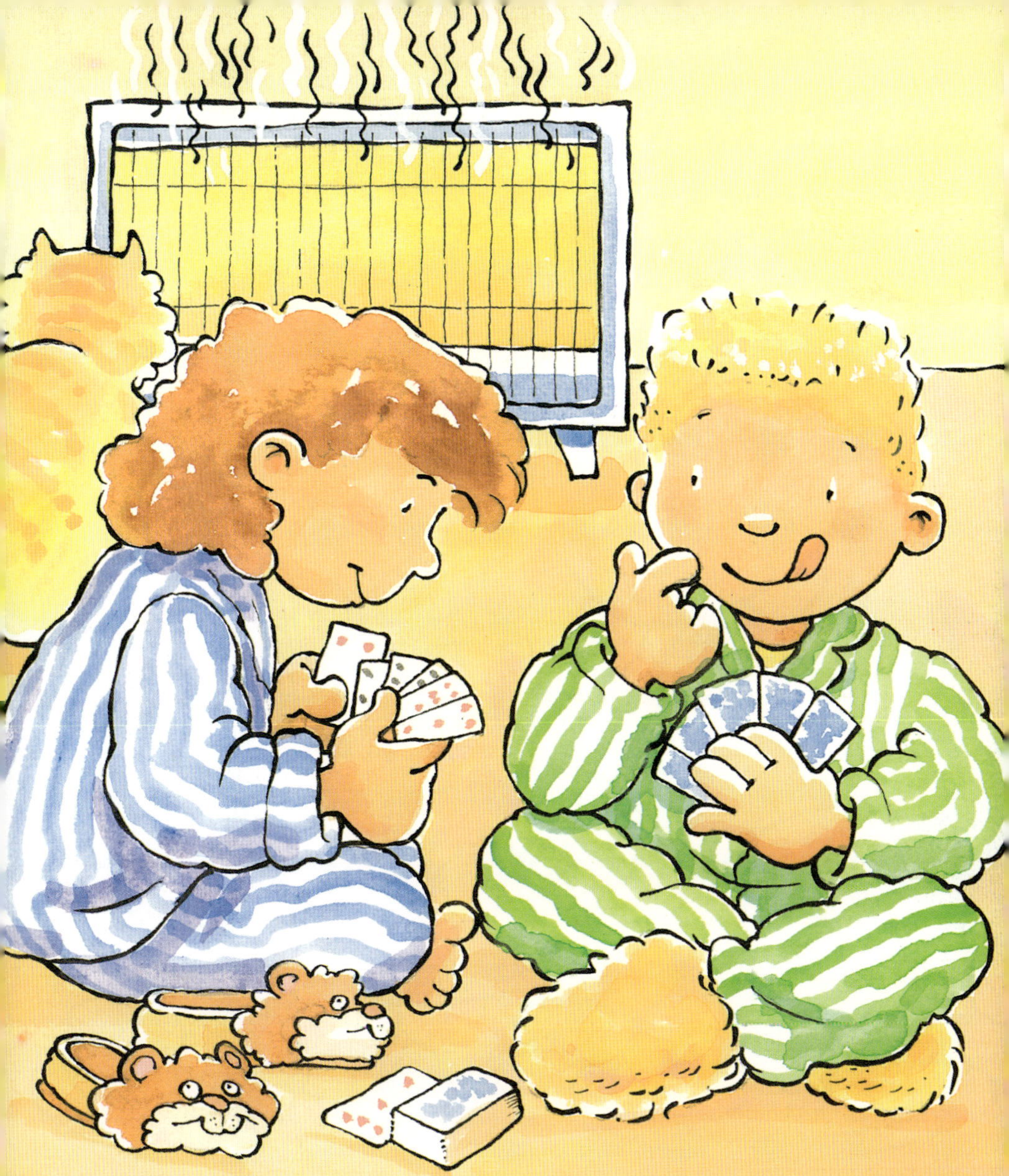

The heater is hot.

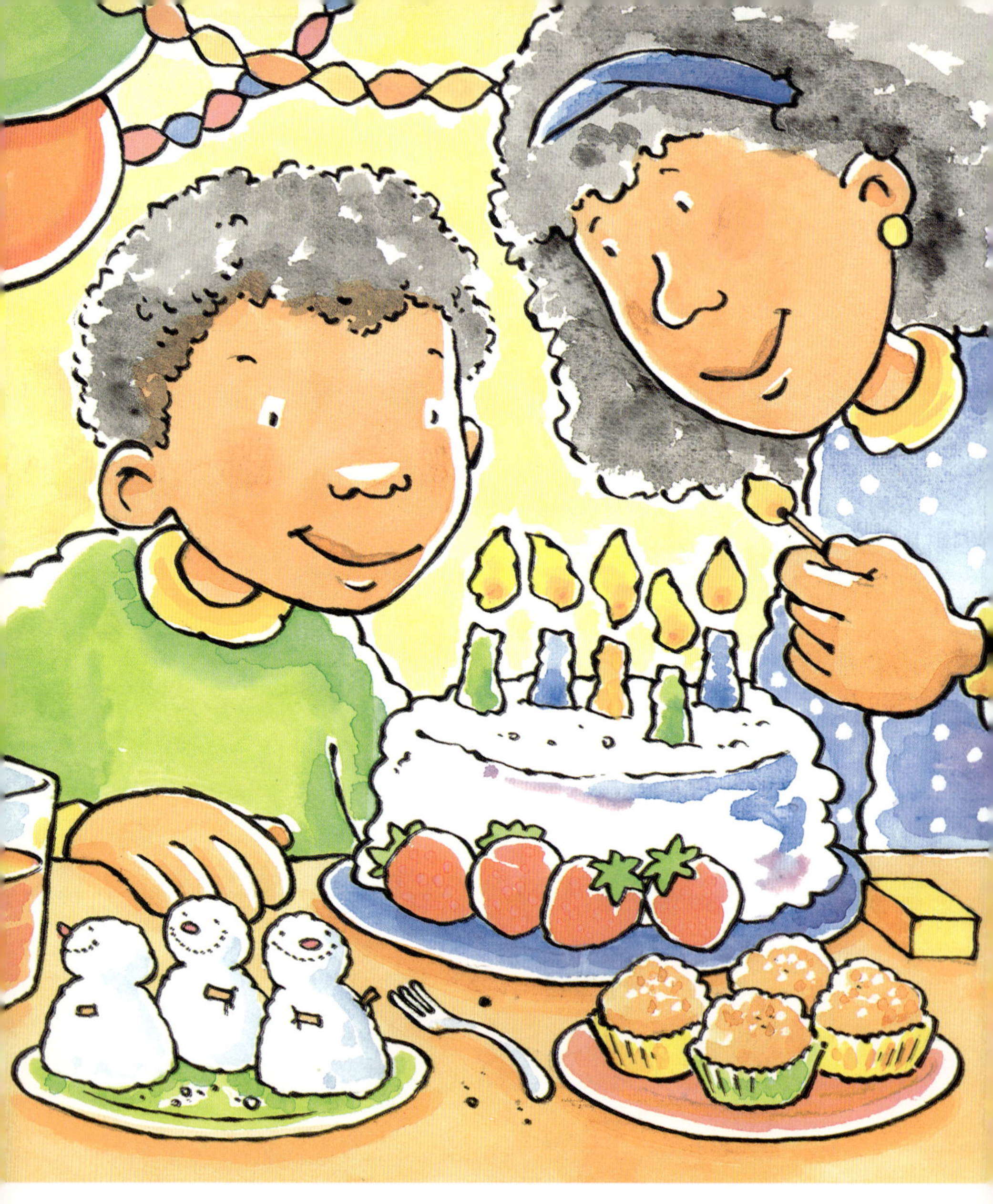

A candle is hot.

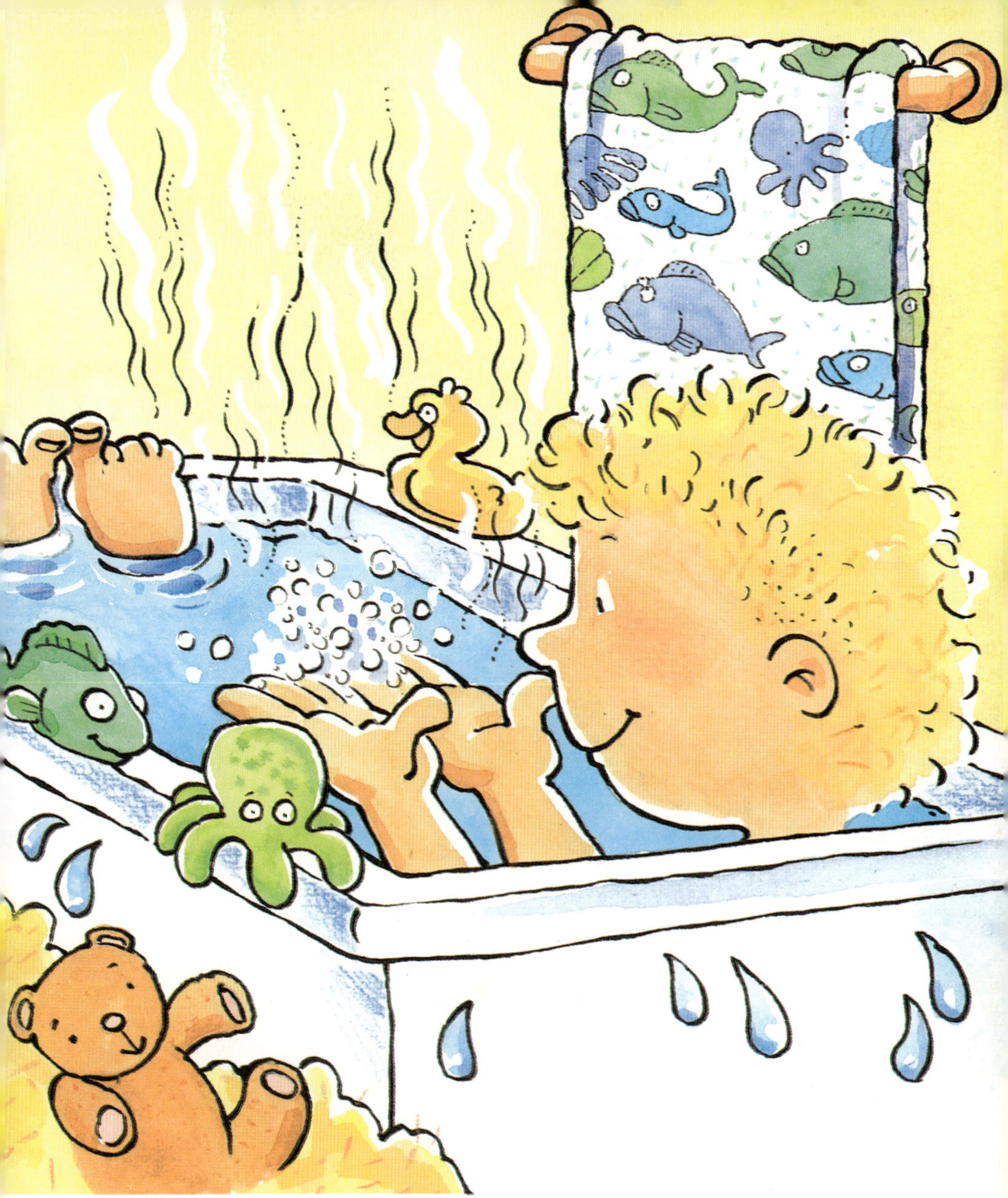

My bath is hot.

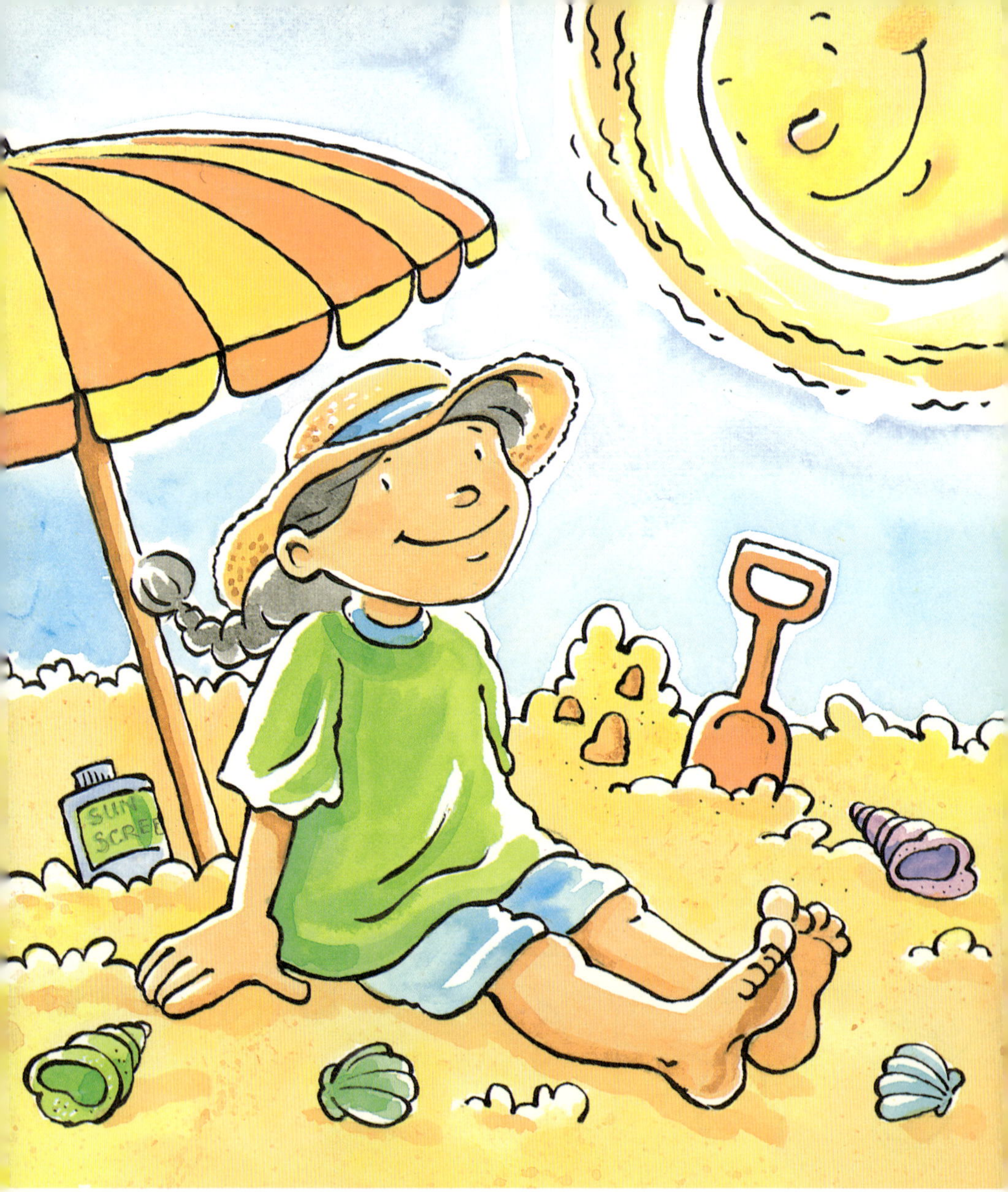

The sun is hot.

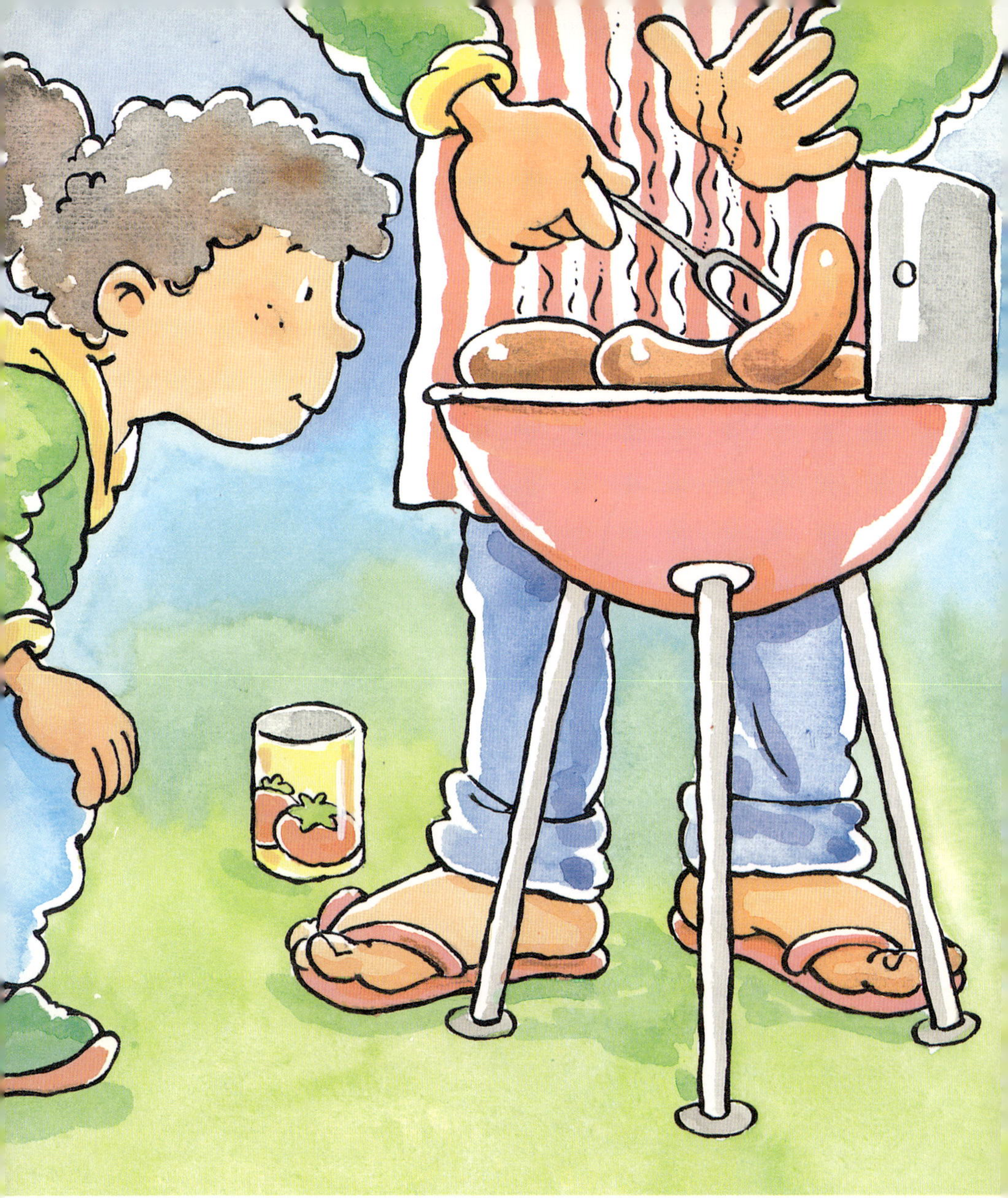

A barbecue is hot.

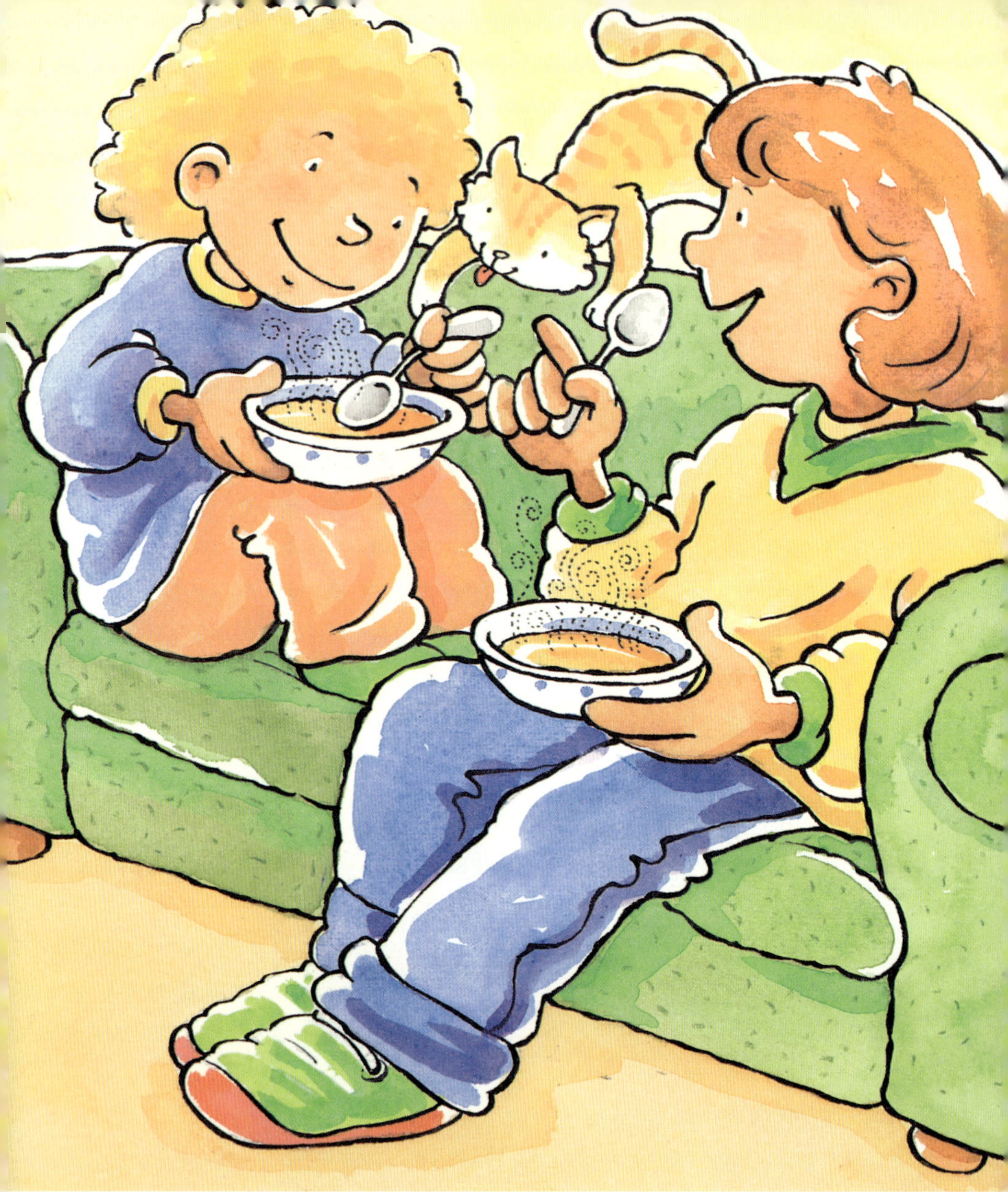

Soup is hot. Yum!